M000208675

To

From

Date

Occasion

BATHED in LOVE

Inspirations to shower you with joy
and soak you in hope

Katherine J. Butler, General Editor

Tyndale House Publishers
Carol Stream, Illinois

LIVING
EXPRESSIONS
COLLECTION

Living Expressions invites you to explore
God's Word in a way that is refreshing to
your spirit and restorative to your soul.

Visit Tyndale online at tyndale.com.

TYNDALE, Tyndale's quill logo, *Living Expressions*, and the Living Expressions
logo are registered trademarks of Tyndale House Ministries.

Bathed in Love: Inspirations to Shower You with Joy and Soak You in Hope

Copyright © 2020 by Ronald A. Beers. All rights reserved.

Adapted from *365 Pocket Promises from the Bible* (ISBN 978-1-4143-6986-0),
copyright © 2012 by Ronald A. Beers.

Unless otherwise noted, cover and interior images are from Shutterstock and are
the property of their respective copyright holders, and all rights are reserved. Rose
pattern copyright © katcreate; gold texture copyright © Katie Harp/Unsplash;
pink background copyright © Baleika Tamara; hexagon pattern copyright
© hoverfly; abstract tiled pattern copyright © fbf; blue paisley copyright ©
Sam2211; blue damask copyright © Irtsya; purple background copyright ©
Katia Karpei; purple abstract copyright © stmaary; yellow tile copyright © facai;
yellow mehendi copyright © Pure Sight lab; branches background copyright ©
ESW; leaves background copyright © Irina Krivoruchko; flower background
copyright © photo-nuke; retro wallpaper copyright © Tristan Tan; red paisley
copyright © DigitalDesigner7; square frame copyright © venimo; round,
hexagon, and diamond borders copyright © Vasya Kobelev; medieval pattern
copyright © Drakonova; victorian frame copyright © Anna Poguliaeva.

Designed by Jacqueline L. Nuñez

Scripture quotations are taken from the *Holy Bible*, New Living Translation,
copyright © 1996, 2004, 2015 by Tyndale House Foundation. Used by
permission of Tyndale House Publishers, Carol Stream, Illinois 60188. All
rights reserved.

For information about special discounts for bulk purchases, please contact
Tyndale House Publishers at csresponse@tyndale.com, or call 1-800-323-9400.

ISBN 978-1-4964-4616-9

Printed in China

26   25   24   23   22   21   20
7   6   5   4   3   2   1

CONTENTS

INTRODUCTION

A TEACHER OF RELIGIOUS LAW once asked Jesus a question that perhaps all of us have wondered at one time or another: What is the greatest commandment? In other words, if there is one thing we need to get right, what would it be? Jesus answered with this: "You must love the LORD your God with all your heart, all your soul, all your mind, and all your strength. . . . [And] love your neighbor as yourself" (Mark 12:30-31).

Jesus wants his followers to have a life bathed in love: love for God, love for their neighbors, and love for themselves. This command is not an easy ask and may even seem impossible. Many of us feel there is little space in our souls to love well as we race through life trying to meet one demand after another.

If this is true for you, then this little book is a great place to begin. Inside are one hundred passages from Scripture that have been carefully selected to encourage and inspire your faith. Following the verses are short devotions to bathe you in love. You'll also find self-care

practices sprinkled throughout the book to help you feel refreshed, relaxed, and reconnected to God.

Before you open this book each time, remember that these devotions aren't meant to become one more item on your to-do list. Our hope and prayer is that each reading will help you sink deeper into God's great promises of love and care for you.

Set aside time to deepen your love for God, for your neighbor, and for yourself. For Jesus has said no other commandment is greater than this.

AN OCEAN OF LOVE

May God our Father and the Lord Jesus Christ give you grace and peace. . . . When you believed in Christ, he identified you as his own by giving you the Holy Spirit, whom he promised long ago. The Spirit is God's guarantee that he will give us the inheritance he promised and that he has purchased us to be his own people.

EPHESIANS 1:2, 13-14

God's love is like a vast ocean. He sends wave after wave of blessings to flow over you. Just as the movement of the ocean is constant, God's blessings are constant, even when you are not aware of them. Scripture is filled with descriptions of the gifts God promises to those who love him, including his presence, his grace, and his peace. He also sends you his Holy Spirit, who opens your eyes to the blessings that surround you every day.

Bathe Yourself in Love

Care for yourself by choosing one activity to help you resist unnecessary hurry: a slow walk, an unrushed conversation, leaving five minutes earlier than normal for an appointment, or letting go of items on your to-do list. Resist multitasking so that you can be more present with others and yourself.

RECEIVE GOD'S GIFTS

This is how God loved the world: He gave his one and only Son, so that everyone who believes in him will not perish but have eternal life.

JOHN 3:16

The greatest gift God offers you is his Son, Jesus. Through Jesus, God gives you not only eternal life but also blessings for today: "love, joy, peace, patience, kindness, goodness, faithfulness, gentleness, and self-control" (Galatians 5:22-23). What makes these gifts so wonderful is that you don't have to work for them or earn them. You simply believe that God has given you his Son and eternal life with him. Then you yield yourself to him and accept these blessings, which no one can take away. Have you received God's wonderful gifts?

Everyone who believes in him will not perish but have eternal life.

TOTAL TRANSFORMATION

Don't copy the behavior and customs of this world, but let God transform you into a new person by changing the way you think. Then you will learn to know God's will for you, which is good and pleasing and perfect.

ROMANS 12:2

Letting God change your thinking will help you live according to his priorities, and the freedom it brings is transforming. Jesus modeled a balance between socializing and solitude, action and reflection, mission and meditation, hard work and rest. This pace allowed him to be guided by God's will instead of human pressures. As you learn the art of a balanced life, you'll realize that God is not calling you to meet every need and volunteer at every opportunity. What a relief! Let the transformation begin.

Let God
transform you
into a new
person.

WASHING AWAY YOUR SINS

If you openly declare that Jesus is Lord and believe in your heart that God raised him from the dead, you will be saved. For it is by believing in your heart that you are made right with God, and it is by openly declaring your faith that you are saved.

ROMANS 10:9-10

This world—this life—is fraught with sadness and tragedy. All of us, unfortunately, contribute to this reality and are victimized by it at the same time. The Bible makes it clear that God longs to rescue the people he made and loves. When you believe in your heart that Jesus died to pay the penalty for your sins and that God resurrected him, and when you confess your sins to him and proclaim your faith to others, you secure your salvation and your place in eternity with God and his people. Have you responded to his call yet? He's waiting for you with open arms.

CONNECT WITH CONVERSATION

The LORD is close to all who call on him,
yes, to all who call on him in truth.

PSALM 145:18

Prayer is an intimate conversation with your
heavenly Father. Through prayer he makes his love
and resources available to you. Just as you enjoy being
with the people you love, you'll learn to enjoy spending time with God the more you get to know him and
understand how much he loves you. Good conversation
includes listening as well as talking, so be sure to allow
time to hear God speak to you. When you listen, he
will make his wisdom and his will known to you.

WORTH FOLLOWING

Commit everything you do to the LORD.
Trust him, and he will help you.

PSALM 37:5

Being committed to God means that you trust him to lead you and do what is best for you. It means resolving to do your best to obey all of God's Word in all areas of your life. When you commit to following God, he commits to leading you. Take comfort and shelter in the Lord Almighty—a leader you can trust.

AN UNCHANGING PROMISE

Whatever is good and perfect is a gift coming down to us from God our Father, who created all the lights in the heavens. He never changes or casts a shifting shadow.

JAMES 1:17

God's character never changes, so he is completely reliable. What great comfort! No matter how your life changes, no matter what new situation you face, God is with you. You can always count on his unchanging promise to take good care of you.

A BRAND-NEW YOU

*Great is his faithfulness; his mercies
begin afresh each morning.*

LAMENTATIONS 3:23

Life is a series of beginnings, and how you enter into them makes all the difference. Although the thought of new beginnings can sometimes make you feel anxious, remember that you experience them all the time. Each day brings a whole series of new opportunities, including chances to get to know God better and to start over with a new attitude toward circumstances and people in your life. God's mercy toward you is new every day, no matter what you've done or how you've treated him or other people the day before. That means you don't have to be burdened by yesterday's failures or regrets.

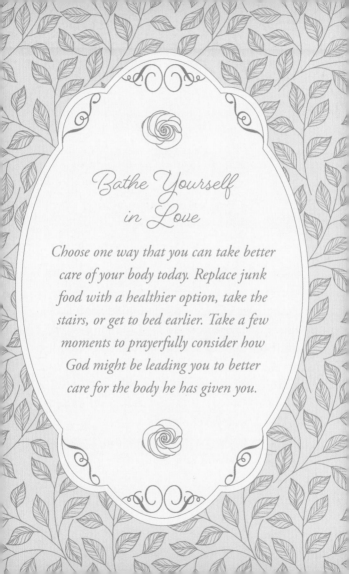

Bathe Yourself in Love

Choose one way that you can take better care of your body today. Replace junk food with a healthier option, take the stairs, or get to bed earlier. Take a few moments to prayerfully consider how God might be leading you to better care for the body he has given you.

THE ADVOCATE

*When the Father sends the Advocate as my representative—
that is, the Holy Spirit—he will teach you everything
and will remind you of everything I have told you.*

JOHN 14:26

Long ago God promised the gift of the Holy
Spirit to his people, but the gift was not given until
after Jesus' resurrection and ascension into heaven.
Anyone who has received Jesus Christ as their Savior
also has the presence of the Holy Spirit in their life.
The Holy Spirit helps you understand the deep truths
of God, convicts you of sin, teaches you how to live
a life that pleases God, helps you pray, enables you to
resist temptation, and assures you that you are a child
of God. Thank God for giving you his Holy Spirit, and
pray expectantly that he will release more and more of
the Spirit's power in your life.

The Holy
Spirit . . . will
teach you
everything.

LIGHT FOR YOUR PATH

*Your word is a lamp to guide my feet
and a light for my path.*

PSALM 119:105

God's guidance is not so much a searchlight that brightens a large area as it is a flashlight that illuminates just enough of the path ahead to show you where to take the next few steps. God has a definite plan for you, but he doesn't usually reveal it all at once. He wants you to learn to trust him each step of the way. As you read the Bible today, ask the Lord to shed a bit of light on an area of your life where you need his guidance. Then, by faith, take a few steps forward. His Word won't lead you astray.

Your word
is a lamp to
guide my feet.

ROCK-SOLID SECURITY

*Those who fear the LORD are secure; he will
be a refuge for their children.*

PROVERBS 14:26

When you daily read and meditate on the
truths of God's Word, you build a solid foundation
that will not easily crack under pressure. Jesus said
that a person who studies and obeys his Word is like
someone who builds his house on solid rock. When a
storm threatens, the house "won't collapse because it is
built on bedrock" (Matthew 7:25). Life's battles may be
strong enough to knock down some of your walls, but
your foundation will remain steady and secure because
God's truths are eternal.

WRAP YOURSELF IN HOPE

*All glory to God, who is able, through his
mighty power at work within us, to accomplish
infinitely more than we might ask or think.*

EPHESIANS 3:20

Most people hope too little in God and expect
too little from him. If you remind yourself of the
amazing things God has already done, you will have
reason to believe that the sovereign Lord of the universe
wants to bless you more abundantly than you can
imagine. Delight in wrapping yourself in this wonderful
hope today.

YOUR TRUE SELF

*You made [human beings] only a little lower than
God and crowned them with glory and honor.*

PSALM 8:5

To have dignity means to understand who God
made you to be—a human being who bears his image.
In the eyes of the Creator, you have great worth and
value, and you have been made for a special purpose.
Your dignity comes not from what others think about
you but from how God sees you. And because your
Creator has made you to reflect his glory and honor,
you can walk into each day with your head held high.
This gives you not only dignity but also the confidence
to boldly serve him wherever he leads you. How can
your God-given sense of dignity give you confidence
and purpose today?

PLAYING YOUR PART

Just as our bodies have many parts and each part has a special function, so it is with Christ's body. We are many parts of one body, and we all belong to each other. In his grace, God has given us different gifts for doing certain things well.

ROMANS 12:4-6

Belonging to God makes you part of Christ's body, the church. The next step is figuring out what part of the body you are: A hand that moves? A foot that steps? An ear that listens? A mouth that speaks? If each of God's children understands his or her part and does it faithfully, the body functions as God intended. When you know what kinds of things you do well, you'll find where you can best serve God and others and gain a sense of purpose and fulfillment. Will you play your part?

SHH . . . LISTEN

When you pray, go away by yourself, shut the door behind you, and pray to your Father in private. Then your Father, who sees everything, will reward you.

MATTHEW 6:6

Sometimes you must be still and alone to hear God speak. Just find a quiet place and tell God you are listening and ready to hear him speak to your heart and mind. Soak in this peaceful time of solitude and fellowship with God. He promises to see you and reward you.

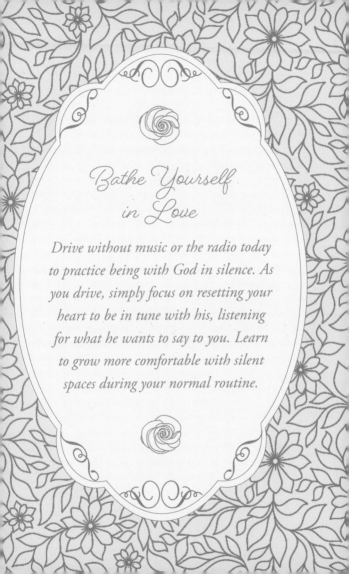

Bathe Yourself in Love

Drive without music or the radio today to practice being with God in silence. As you drive, simply focus on resetting your heart to be in tune with his, listening for what he wants to say to you. Learn to grow more comfortable with silent spaces during your normal routine.

ENJOY THE CELEBRATION

The LORD your God is living among you. He is
a mighty savior. He will take delight in you with
gladness. With his love, he will calm all your fears.
He will rejoice over you with joyful songs.

ZEPHANIAH 3:17

The Lord rejoices and celebrates when his
people faithfully follow him. If you trust his ways and
obey his commands, the God of the universe will liter-
ally sing songs of joy because of you! He's delighted
and glad that you're his child. On this day, choose to
enjoy the love, peace, and security that such a good
Father brings.

Bathe Yourself in Love

Set an alarm on your phone or place a note in your home as a simple reminder that God is with you and delights in you. When you see the reminder, pause for a few moments and say to him, "Thank you for seeing me and delighting in me."

KINDNESS SO DEEP

The LORD is merciful and compassionate, slow to get angry and filled with unfailing love. . . . The LORD is righteous in everything he does; he is filled with kindness.

PSALM 145:8, 17

God promises to give you mercy when you don't deserve it, to be patient and not lash out in anger when you do something wrong. In other words, he promises to love you unconditionally, even when you don't return his love. God didn't just create kindness; he is kindness. Everything he does for you is an act of kindness. He wants you to become everything he created you to be and gives you every opportunity to experience the joy of fellowship with him. Treat yourself today to the many reminders of God's kindness in your life.

The LORD
. . . is filled with
kindness.

HEALTHY MOTIVATION

Pay careful attention to your own work, for then you will get the satisfaction of a job well done, and you won't need to compare yourself to anyone else.

GALATIANS 6:4

People often get stressed out when they take on activities and responsibilities for the wrong reasons. As you consider upcoming involvements, ask God to help you do things with the right motives and to reveal any that might be unhealthy. Then you can better decide which activities to commit to and which ones to avoid. When you say yes with the right motivation, you'll be able to work with passion and purpose, bringing great satisfaction and fulfillment.

Get the
satisfaction
of a job
well done.

RELAX INTO GOD'S COUNSEL

*To those who listen to my teaching, more
understanding will be given, and they will
have an abundance of knowledge.*

MATTHEW 13:12

In an age of conflicting claims and confusing
information, everyone is anxiously looking for guidance. Maybe that's why counselors are in such great
demand and advice columns are so common. But
there is a critical difference between worldly advice
and godly counsel. God's wisdom is best because he is
all-knowing. Through his Word, God—the one who
knows everything that will happen today and tomorrow
and in the future—wants you to relax in the knowledge
that leads to understanding. Then you will have the
wisdom to weigh and interpret advice from others.

SINK INTO THE TRUTH

*The LORD is compassionate and merciful, slow
to get angry and filled with unfailing love.*

PSALM 103:8

Your beliefs about God are more important
than any other beliefs you have. If you believe that God
is always angry with you, you will likely be defensive,
fearful, or antagonistic toward him. But when you
believe that God shows you deep love and grace, you
can live in the joy of knowing that you're forgiven and
will live in his presence forever. You will no longer fear
God's retribution but will thank him for his grace. Sink
down deep into the truth about God's character and let
his love wash over you. Then you will "constantly speak
his praises" (Psalm 34:1) because of his goodness!

SURROUNDED BY MIRACLES

*Shout joyful praises to God, all the earth! Sing
about the glory of his name! Tell the world how
glorious he is. Say to God, "How awesome are your
deeds!" . . . Come and see what our God has done,
what awesome miracles he performs for people!*

PSALM 66:1-3, 5

God works on behalf of his people in miraculous
ways. The news is filled with all the terrible things that
are happening in the world; but if you step back for
a moment, you can begin to get a glimpse of God's
hand quietly working miracles in many people's lives—
including yours—every day. His hand is there, even
when you don't see it.

THE BEAUTY OF HUMILITY

*All of you, dress yourselves in humility as you
relate to one another, for "God opposes the
proud but gives grace to the humble."*

1 PETER 5:5

True humility results from understanding
who you are and who God is. When you are sick
or injured and must rely on a physician's care, you
are humbled because you realize your vulnerability.
Likewise, you are humbled when you realize you're
completely dependent on God to heal your soul. When
you have this kind of humility, you'll be happy to serve
your Lord in any way he asks—and with the beauty
of a gracious spirit. Do you have the humility to serve
God wherever he is calling you?

SIMPLY ABIDING

*Remain in me, and I will remain in you. For a branch
cannot produce fruit if it is severed from the vine, and
you cannot be fruitful unless you remain in me. Yes,
I am the vine; you are the branches. Those who remain
in me, and I in them, will produce much fruit.*

JOHN 15:4-5

When you spend time with Jesus, he fills you
with his Spirit of grace, love, and power. The result is
that your simple acts of service are transformed into
profound and purposeful expressions of his heart. He
can turn your gift of singing into a chorus of praise that
ministers to an entire congregation. He can turn your
casually shared testimony of faith into a life-changing
moment for a friend. How comforting that Jesus
doesn't ask you to conjure up great acts of faith. He
only desires that you abide in his presence. From that
place of intimacy, you will "produce much fruit."

Bathe Yourself in Love

Schedule a time to take a walk alone with the Lord today—even if it's only for five minutes. Picture him walking beside you. Resist the urge to fill the time with any sounds or words, and just enjoy being in God's company.

CLOSE YOUR EYES FOR A MOMENT

We live with great expectation, and we have a price-
less inheritance—an inheritance that is kept in heaven
for you, pure and undefiled, beyond the reach of change
and decay. And through your faith, God is protect-
ing you by his power until you receive this salvation,
which is ready to be revealed on the last day for all to
see. So be truly glad. There is wonderful joy ahead, even
though you must endure many trials for a little while.

1 PETER 1:3-6

When you focus on a fixed point in the distance, it motivates you to move in a straight line toward
your goal. In the same way, as a follower of Jesus, you
must fix your eyes on heaven. As you do so, the hope
you have for your "priceless inheritance" will help you
endure the discomforts and trials of daily life. Close
your eyes for a moment and "be truly glad" as you
imagine the glory and joy that's yet to come.

God is
protecting you
by his power.

THE BALM OF ENCOURAGEMENT

I praise your name for your unfailing love and faithfulness; for your promises are backed by all the honor of your name. As soon as I pray, you answer me; you encourage me by giving me strength.

PSALM 138:2-3

With each new day comes the need for a fresh dose of encouragement. It's easy to focus on the problems in front of us instead of seeing that God is standing by to help us overcome them. Looking at our circumstances instead of focusing on God can bring discouragement, and doubting God's love will only draw us away from our greatest source of help. Today, be encouraged that God gives you strength and helps you succeed as you trust in him. Run to the Lord in prayer; he promises to hear, answer, and soothe you with the balm of his encouragement.

You encourage
me by giving
me strength.

YOU'RE NEVER ALONE

*The LORD your God . . . will neither
fail you nor abandon you.*

DEUTERONOMY 31:6

In the dark hours of the night, do you feel
desperately alone and rejected? Perhaps a best friend
deserted you, the marriage you hoped for never
materialized, or the person you're married to now
wants out. Maybe your child has turned against you or
your parents and friends don't seem to care about you.
But God says, "Do not be afraid, for I am with you"
(Isaiah 43:5). He, too, was "acquainted with deepest
grief" (Isaiah 53:3). The Lord promises to love you and
stay with you no matter what.

DISPLAY YOUR BEAUTY

People judge by outward appearance,
but the LORD looks at the heart.

1 SAMUEL 16:7

Our eyes are trained to first assess others based on their physical appearance. Society makes us believe that an unappealing face equals an unattractive person, no matter how beautiful they are on the inside. But God sees into the heart. To him, real beauty comes from who he made you to be and the ways you are living for him, not what you look like. Display your beauty today through acts of kindness and faith.

A BEACON OF HOPE

You are a chosen people. You are royal priests, a holy nation, God's very own possession. As a result, you can show others the goodness of God, for he called you out of the darkness into his wonderful light.

1 PETER 2:9

Have you ever searched through drawers and closets for a flashlight, only to discover upon finding it that its batteries were dead? Although the flashlight had the potential to provide light, without new batteries it was useless. You, like every believer, have within you the light of Christ and the potential to shine upon others and draw them to God. God promises that you will do amazing things if you only let him work through you. So don't be afraid to let your light shine. Become a beacon of hope to those around you.

TAP INTO GOD'S EXPERTISE

If you need wisdom, ask our generous God, and he will give it to you. He will not rebuke you for asking.

JAMES 1:5

When you're faced with a decision, you may be afraid to ask God for his wisdom and insight because you think he has bigger things to worry about. Not so. God *wants* to help you because he loves you. And he cares about your little decisions just as much as he does your big ones. When you bring your heart's concerns to God, he shares his wisdom with you. Tap into his expertise and reap the rewards of knowing him.

PASSIONATE PURSUIT

*Long ago the LORD said . . . "I have loved
you, my people, with an everlasting love. With
unfailing love I have drawn you to myself."*

JEREMIAH 31:3

God created you, loves you, and longs to have
a relationship with you, so he pursues you with
persistent and unfailing love. Scripture is filled with
imagery of the Lord seeking out his people. Ezekiel
34:11 promises, "I myself will search and find my
sheep," and Luke 19:10 says, "The Son of Man came
to seek and save those who are lost." Has he caught
your attention yet? Take great comfort in knowing that
the God of the universe pursues you with passion.

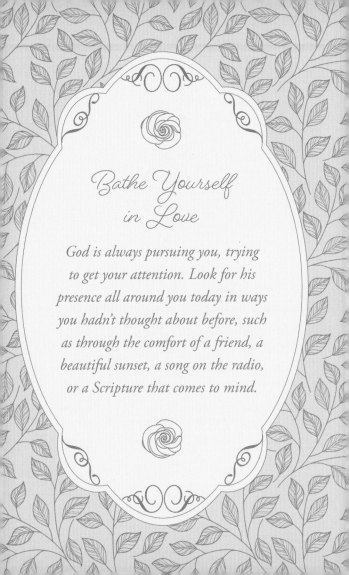

Bathe Yourself
in Love

*God is always pursuing you, trying
to get your attention. Look for his
presence all around you today in ways
you hadn't thought about before, such
as through the comfort of a friend, a
beautiful sunset, a song on the radio,
or a Scripture that comes to mind.*

ON CALL RESPITE

Jesus said, "Come to me, all of you who are weary and carry heavy burdens, and I will give you rest. Take my yoke upon you. Let me teach you, because I am humble and gentle at heart, and you will find rest for your souls. For my yoke is easy to bear, and the burden I give you is light."

MATTHEW 11:28-30

When you visit friends who live far away, you usually have the privilege of enjoying a room they've prepared for your comfort and rest. God does the same for you: When you come to him for spiritual refreshment, he welcomes you into a place where you can feel safe and rest quietly. In his presence, the burdens of the world are put into perspective. Today, will you go to the Creator of rest and linger with him?

Bathe Yourself in Love

Write down three areas in which you can practice restraint this week and embrace rest. For example, you could (1) say no to a social engagement, (2) skip an unnecessary errand, or (3) choose not to take work home. Think about how it might feel to refrain from those activities and to rest instead.

PRAY CONTINUALLY

*I love the LORD because he hears my voice and
my prayer for mercy. Because he bends down to
listen, I will pray as long as I have breath!*

PSALM 116:1-2

God listens carefully to you and answers every
prayer. His answer may be *yes*, *no*, or *wait*, just as loving
parents might give any of these responses when their
child makes a request. If God answered *yes* every time,
he would spoil you and endanger your well-being.
Saying *no* to each request would be vindictive, stingy,
and hard on your spirit. Always answering *wait* would
frustrate you. God answers your prayers according
to what he knows is best for you. Knowing that God
listens and responds can inspire you to pray continually,
even when his answer isn't the one you wanted.

I will pray
as long as
I have breath!

EXPRESS YOUR CREATIVITY

*We are God's masterpiece. He has created us
anew in Christ Jesus, so we can do the good
things he planned for us long ago.*

EPHESIANS 2:10

Creativity is built into every human being.
And since God made you, you are also a product of
his creativity! God wants you to use the unique gifts
he fashioned in you to serve others. You can express
yourself—and worship the Lord—in potentially
hundreds of different ways: singing, playing a musical
instrument, crafting things, thinking through problems,
or loving and helping others. Enjoy expressing your
creativity in God-honoring ways, because it is an exten-
sion of a characteristic of God. As God's child, you, too,
can reflect God's creative nature to the world.

We are God's
masterpiece.

BOUNDLESS ASSISTANCE

The LORD is my strength and shield. I trust him with
all my heart. He helps me, and my heart is filled
with joy. I burst out in songs of thanksgiving.

PSALM 28:7

When you ask God to help your endeavors
and trust that he will, you open a lifeline to the God
who loves to do the impossible. Over and over again,
Scripture emphasizes how the Lord delights in giving
his people strength and guidance. You will be filled with
joy and thanksgiving when you see the amazing things
God has planned for you!

ANTICIPATE GOOD THINGS

"I know the plans I have for you," says the
LORD. "They are plans for good and not for
disaster, to give you a future and a hope."

JEREMIAH 29:11

Many people picture God as stern and
vindictive, just watching and waiting for the chance
to zap humans with bolts of misfortune. But this verse
illustrates the opposite: God loves you and wants only
good things for you. He wants your future—both in
this life and in heaven—to be bright and hopeful.
Today, give yourself some much-needed therapy. Allow
your mind and heart to anticipate a joyful and hope-
filled future.

REINFORCED WITH GOD'S POWER

All glory to God, who is able, through his
mighty power at work within us, to accomplish
infinitely more than we might ask or think.

EPHESIANS 3:20

God's knowledge is unlimited, and yet he created each of us with limitations. He did not do this to discourage you but to help you realize your utter need for him. It is in your weakness that God's strength shines the brightest. When you accomplish something great despite your limitations, it's obvious that God was working through you and deserves the credit. Jesus says, "What is impossible for people is possible with God" (Luke 18:27). The next time you become frustrated with your limitations, thank God for the opportunity to see him demonstrate his power. As he works through you, together you will accomplish more than you ever could have dreamed.

REFLECTIONS OF HOLINESS

Even before he made the world, God loved us and chose us in Christ to be holy and without fault in his eyes.

EPHESIANS 1:4

God does not regard you as holy because you are sinless but because Jesus died to take the punishment for your sins and gave you his own holiness. Only Jesus lived a sinless life, but anyone who seeks forgiveness for their sins and acknowledges Jesus as their Savior and Lord receives Christ's own righteousness. Because of Jesus' sacrifice, God views that person as holy. What an amazing thought! When God looks at you, he sees only the reflection of Christ's holiness. Thank him now for "this gift too wonderful for words" (2 Corinthians 9:15).

LIVING WITH HEAVEN IN MIND

There is more than enough room in my Father's home. If this were not so, would I have told you that I am going to prepare a place for you?

JOHN 14:2

When contemplating the end of your life's journey, you can take great comfort in knowing that not only is there a heaven, but Jesus is also making preparations there for your arrival. Heaven is more than a paradise you will visit only on vacation. It's an eternal dwelling place where you will live in joyful fellowship with your heavenly Father and your heavenly family. Though death is a great unknown, Jesus Christ has gone before you, and he is preparing a glorious place for you to stay. If you know and love Jesus, you can be confident that your room is ready and waiting.

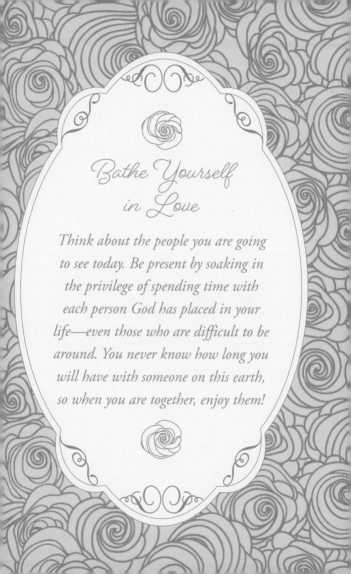

Bathe Yourself in Love

Think about the people you are going to see today. Be present by soaking in the privilege of spending time with each person God has placed in your life—even those who are difficult to be around. You never know how long you will have with someone on this earth, so when you are together, enjoy them!

FOREVER CHANGED

Anyone who belongs to Christ has become a new person. The old life is gone; a new life has begun!

2 CORINTHIANS 5:17

The Bible teaches two great truths about change. The first is that despite the changing world around us, God is changeless and dependable. The second is that when we choose to follow God, we experience an inner change of heart (repentance) that produces an outward change of lifestyle (obedience). When your heart is changed by God's truth and love, your life will be changed forever.

*A new life
has begun!*

LOVE COMPREHENDED

*Love is patient and kind. Love is not jealous or boastful
or proud or rude. It does not demand its own way. It is
not irritable, and it keeps no record of being wronged.
It does not rejoice about injustice but rejoices whenever the
truth wins out. Love never gives up, never loses faith, is
always hopeful, and endures through every circumstance.*

1 CORINTHIANS 13:4-7

These well-known verses are some of the
most eloquent and accurate descriptions of love ever
written. Contrary to popular opinion, true love is first
of all a courageous commitment and an unwavering
choice to care for another person. In turn, this love
produces powerful feelings. You can't practice the
qualities and behaviors described in these verses in your
own strength, but if you keep in step with the Holy
Spirit, you'll walk in love and experience the satisfaction
and fulfillment that it brings.

Love never
gives up.

THE HARMONY OF DIVERSITY

Live in harmony and peace. Then the God of love and peace will be with you.

2 CORINTHIANS 13:11

One of our greatest challenges is remembering that God intentionally created each person with unique gifts and talents, likes and dislikes—and then focusing on how those differences can help us work together. We must not allow our diversity to set us against each other. Instead, it should bring us together to accomplish more than we ever thought possible. When you and other Christians use your differences in harmony, God promises to live among you and bless you with peace.

TRUE PLEASURE

*God is working in you, giving you the desire
and the power to do what pleases him.*

PHILIPPIANS 2:13

You probably already know from experience that
God doesn't force change on anyone. Still, if you try to
become a better person in your own strength, you will
get discouraged. Instead, ask God to begin a work of
transformation in you that will last a lifetime. When
you put Jesus first, you give him permission to change
you by making your heart more like his. Allow God's
Spirit to do the work for you. "It is not by force nor by
strength, but by my Spirit, says the LORD of Heaven's
Armies" (Zechariah 4:6). His desires will become your
desires, resulting in dramatic changes in your life that
are pleasing to him—and ultimately to you as well.

PRICELESS IN HIS EYES

What is the price of two sparrows—one copper coin?
But not a single sparrow can fall to the ground without
your Father knowing it. . . . So don't be afraid; you are
more valuable to God than a whole flock of sparrows.

MATTHEW 10:29, 31

Deep within every human heart lies a hunger
for significance. We want our lives to count, to make
a difference, to be worth something. Yet many people
carry deep feelings of insignificance. Their lives are
dominated by their inabilities rather than their abilities.
Everywhere they look, they see others who are more
successful, more gifted, more this or that. The Bible,
however, says that every person has great value. You are
significant not because of anything you can accomplish
on your own but because God loves you and redeemed
you with Christ's priceless blood. Never doubt your
extravagant worth.

ADORNED WITH PATIENCE

The Holy Spirit produces this kind of fruit in our lives: love, joy, peace, patience, kindness, goodness, faithfulness, gentleness, and self-control.

GALATIANS 5:22-23, EMPHASIS ADDED

If you've ever spent two hours stuck in rush-hour traffic or held a crying baby at two o'clock in the morning, you know something about patience. According to the Bible, patience is a form of perseverance and endurance that allows you to respond to frustrating circumstances with grace and self-control. Patience is not merely a personality trait; it's a by-product of the presence and work of the Holy Spirit in the hearts and minds of believers. God promises that when the Holy Spirit is in you, he will produce more patience in your life. So take a deep breath and thank the Lord for filling you with his Spirit. When he's got *you*, he's got *this*—no matter how difficult the situation.

DEEPLY ROOTED

*Blessed are those who . . . have made the LORD their
hope and confidence. They are like trees planted along
a riverbank, with roots that reach deep into the water.
Such trees are not bothered by the heat or worried by long
months of drought. . . . They never stop producing fruit.*

JEREMIAH 17:7-8

God uses your circumstances, good or bad, to help
you—and others—grow. It's easy to be joyful and faithful when life is going well, but when life gets tough,
believers have a unique opportunity to demonstrate
how a relationship with God brings comfort, confidence, and hope. When you seek God in the most difficult of circumstances, three wonderful things happen:
(1) You learn to rely on God instead of yourself,
(2) others are blessed by seeing your faith and hope in
action, and (3) you deepen your roots in the nourishment of God's love, allowing you to thrive even through
extended trials.

Bathe Yourself in Love

Plan a shopping trip today or tomorrow to buy a plant for your home. As you water and care for this plant, allow it to be a continual reminder of God's tender care for you amid difficult circumstances.

REJUVENATING WORDS

The instructions of the LORD are perfect,
reviving the soul. The decrees of the LORD
are trustworthy, making wise the simple.

PSALM 19:7

Did you know that simply reading and meditating on the Bible revives your soul? God's words are living, and therefore they are relevant to your current situation, no matter what it is. The almighty God speaks to you through the Bible, and his words bring peace, strength, comfort, wisdom, and hope—the very nourishment you need for revival. Sin starves your soul, but God's Word rejuvenates it.

Bathe Yourself in Love

Slowly read through a psalm today. Read it
as if God were speaking its words directly
to you. Afterward, take time to pause
and listen. Pray, "God, what might you
want to say to me through this passage?"

PAYING IT FORWARD

*Let everything you say be good and helpful, so that your
words will be an encouragement to those who hear them.*

EPHESIANS 4:29

The Lord himself encourages us when we
meditate on his Word and spend time with him in
prayer. But he's also pleased when his children encourage each other. When we've run aground, our brothers
and sisters in Christ can help us regain commitment,
courage, and hope. They can help us love and live
again. And don't forget to pay it forward. Romans
12:8 says, "If your gift is to encourage others, be
encouraging." Encouragement is a beautiful gift that
brings renewal. When you encourage others, you
will bring them a divine blessing as well as receive a
blessing yourself.

Let everything
you say be good
and helpful.

REVITALIZING ASSURANCE

If we are faithful to the end, trusting God just as firmly as when we first believed, we will share in all that belongs to Christ.

HEBREWS 3:14

Once Jesus becomes your Savior and Lord, you are saved from God's rightful judgment. How can you be sure of this? Because God promised, and God always keeps his promises. And although your relationship with Jesus as Savior and Lord began at a particular moment in time, he desires an active, growing friendship with you. When you maintain this kind of relationship with him on a daily basis, you can rest assured that you will enjoy eternal life with the Lord and receive eternal rewards as well.

We will share
in all that belongs
to Christ.

FAILURE ISN'T AN OPTION

The LORD directs the steps of the godly. He delights in every detail of their lives. Though they stumble, they will never fall, for the LORD holds them by the hand.

PSALM 37:23-24

Don't let failure get you down! Get up and try again. Many inspiring success stories tell of people who failed many times but never gave up. Most important, never give up on your relationship with God. He promises you the ultimate success of knowing him personally and gaining eternal life.

FILLED WITH COMPASSION

Moved with compassion, Jesus reached out and touched him. "I am willing," he said. "Be healed!"

MARK 1:41

Compassion is both an emotion (feeling concern for someone) and an action (doing something to meet their need). The stories in the Bible where Jesus showed compassion toward those he encountered give us a small glimpse of the compassion God has for us. Let them remind you that he sees you, cares about your hurt, and is ready to meet the deep needs in your heart. Will you call out to him today?

HE NEVER FALTERS

Faith shows the reality of what we hope for;
it is the evidence of things we cannot see.

HEBREWS 11:1

If you ever begin to lose confidence in God's ability to work in a situation, go right to the Bible. As you read about the promises he has already fulfilled, you'll develop greater faith that he will also fulfill his promises for the future. Numbers 23:19 says, "God is not a man, so he does not lie. He is not human, so he does not change his mind. Has he ever spoken and failed to act? Has he ever promised and not carried it through?" Rest today in the confidence and hope that our God does not falter, that his faithful ways never fail.

REST IN CONTENTMENT

By his divine power, God has given us everything we
need for living a godly life. We have received all of
this by coming to know him, the one who called us to
himself by means of his marvelous glory and excellence.

2 PETER 1:3

When your contentment depends on
having what you want, you'll become unhappy if you
don't get it. When your contentment comes from Jesus
meeting your needs, security and happiness will follow.
Watch your contentment grow as you trust that God
is in control and is working out his wonderful plan for
your life.

ALL THE PLACES YOU'LL GO

*May the LORD . . . grant your heart's desires
and make all your plans succeed.*

PSALM 20:1, 4

Before a ship sets out on a long voyage, the captain needs to plot the course. This includes choosing the route, setting the schedule, determining the places to stop, and deciding on the responsibilities for each crew member. By planning ahead and setting attainable goals, the captain seeks to ensure that the ship will stay on the right course and arrive safely at its destination. The same principle is true for you. Goals help give you direction in life, and setting small, attainable goals is necessary to determine your course. When God is your captain and companion, you will stay on track and succeed. Ultimately, he promises to safely guide you to your final destination—the Kingdom of Heaven in all its glory and perfection.

Bathe Yourself
in Love

What activities most refresh you and
connect you with God? For the sake of
your soul, give yourself permission today
or this week to engage in a restful practice
or meet with an uplifting person.

A TOTAL MAKEOVER

I will give you a new heart, and I will put a new spirit in you. I will take out your stony, stubborn heart and give you a tender, responsive heart.

EZEKIEL 36:26

When you give God control of your life, he gives you a new heart, a new nature, and a new desire to please him. God renews you when you humble yourself before him, turn away from sinful habits, and make a daily effort to connect with him. As you do these things, your love for God will grow. He can change even the hardest heart of stone into an obedient and loving heart. Are you willing to let him change you?

I will put a new
spirit in you.

83

STEADFAST LOYALTY

Never let loyalty and kindness leave you! Tie them around your neck as a reminder. Write them deep within your heart. Then you will find favor with both God and people, and you will earn a good reputation.

PROVERBS 3:3-4

Loyalty can be defined as a highly personal form of commitment. Loyalty says, "No matter what happens around us or between us, there is no fear, doubt, or hurt that can make me turn my back on you." When you have loyalty in a relationship, it is secure and solid. When you do not, the relationship is filled with insecurity and fear. The Bible teaches that loyalty is part of the very character of God. You communicate your loyalty to God by seeking to obey his Word and admitting to him when you've fallen short, and he expresses his loyalty by refusing to give up on you, no matter what.

The LORD leads
with unfailing love
and faithfulness.

COURAGE FOR WHATEVER COMES

Don't be afraid, for I am with you. Don't be discouraged,
for I am your God. I will strengthen you and help you.
I will hold you up with my victorious right hand.

ISAIAH 41:10

To experience fear is normal. To be paralyzed
by fear, however, can be an indication that you doubt
God's promises or his ability to care for you in the face
of danger. Realize that courage doesn't come from your
qualifications or your credentials but from the promise
of God's presence and power. Jesus said, "The peace I
give is a gift the world cannot give. So don't be troubled
or afraid" (John 14:27). When you know God is with
you and helping you, you have peace that can face any
fear.

RICH REWARDS

No eye has seen, no ear has heard, and no mind has imagined what God has prepared for those who love him.

1 CORINTHIANS 2:9

You may wonder, since Christians suffer like everybody else, why bother living for God? If all we had to live for were the rewards of this life, then a "why bother" attitude might be understandable. But the Bible is clear that those who trust Jesus Christ to forgive their sins receive the amazing promise of eternal life. In addition, when you seek to obey God, your relationships are fulfilling, your life displays integrity, and your conscience is clear. Despite trials and tribulations, your faithfulness still results in rewards in this life; and your heavenly rewards will be greater than you can imagine.

ONE STEP AT A TIME

Be tenderhearted, and keep a humble attitude.
Don't repay evil for evil. Don't retaliate with
insults when people insult you. Instead, pay them
back with a blessing. That is what God has called
you to do, and he will grant you his blessing.

1 PETER 3:8-9

While it's good to set big goals for family,
career, or personal achievements, it's also important
to set smaller daily goals. You can determine today
to be kind toward others, to be humble, to respond
gracefully even when someone takes advantage of you,
to read your Bible, and to say an encouraging word.
These practices bring great rewards over a lifetime. God
promises to bless you for such small steps of obedience
to him, for they are the essential building blocks of the
bigger things that God wants you to accomplish—and
the blessings you'll receive in return.

YOUR DIVINE PURPOSE

*I have come down from heaven to do the will
of God who sent me, not to do my own will.*

JOHN 6:38

Your greatest hope is that because of Jesus, you
will live forever in God's Kingdom. Until that hope is
fulfilled, God has a plan for you to carry out in your
life here and now. Listen to God and follow him closely
so that you can fulfill his plan for you, just as Jesus
fulfilled God's plan for him. Ask the Lord each day to
reveal his plans for you, and never lose hope that he is
working out his purposes in your life. If you've submit-
ted your will to his, you can be sure he's doing just that,
even if you're not sure what his purposes for you are.
His love won't let you down.

THANKSGIVING THERAPY

Giving thanks is a sacrifice that truly honors me. If you keep to my path, I will reveal to you the salvation of God.

PSALM 50:23

The Bible says that thanking God is a sacrifice that honors him. It recognizes his mercy, provision, and blessing in your life. A thankful heart gives you a positive attitude because it keeps you focused on all God is doing for you instead of what you think you lack. Give thanks to God every day—he promises to bless you with his salvation.

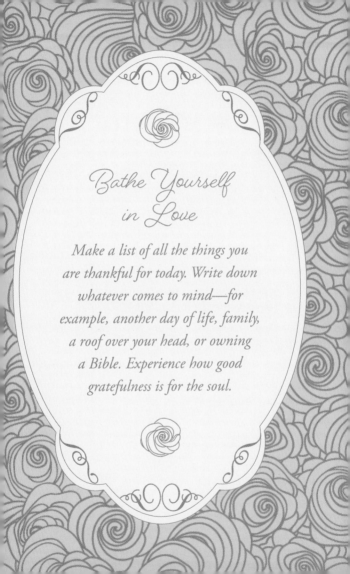

Bathe Yourself in Love

Make a list of all the things you are thankful for today. Write down whatever comes to mind—for example, another day of life, family, a roof over your head, or owning a Bible. Experience how good gratefulness is for the soul.

AN AMPLE SUPPLY

Your heavenly Father already knows all your needs.
Seek the Kingdom of God above all else, and live
righteously, and he will give you everything you need.

MATTHEW 6:32-33

Throughout its pages, the Bible makes it clear that God provides for those who seek him. Jesus himself promises that when we pursue God, he will supply all our needs. Sometimes our definition of our needs is different from God's, so it's a good idea to study his Word and discover what God says we need in order to have fulfilling lives. Today, relish the ample supply of resources that your heavenly Father makes available to you as his child.

Bathe Yourself
in Love

Today, linger at the table longer than you normally would. Take time to smell, taste, and enjoy your food. Allow this exercise to remind you how slowing down helps you better appreciate God's gifts in the moment.

SPIRITUAL NOURISHMENT

Let your roots grow down into him, and let your lives be built on him. Then your faith will grow strong in the truth you were taught, and you will overflow with thankfulness.

COLOSSIANS 2:7

Spiritual growth is like physical growth—you start small and grow one day at a time. As you grow, you need more nourishment. You get physical nourishment by eating healthy foods, and you receive spiritual nourishment by challenging your mind in the study of God's Word, asking questions about it, and seeking answers through prayer and the counsel and experience of other believers. Look at each day as a stepping-stone, and before you know it, you'll be on your way to spiritual maturity and a thankful heart.

Let your lives
be built on him.

GOD IS BESIDE YOU

Be strong and courageous! Do not be afraid or discouraged.
For the LORD your God is with you wherever you go.

JOSHUA 1:9

True courage comes from understanding that
God is stronger than your biggest problem and fiercest
enemy and that he uses his power to help you. Instead
of misplaced confidence in your own strength, courage
is well-placed confidence in *God's strength*. While fear
comes from feeling alone against a great threat, courage comes from knowing that God is beside you and
helping you to fight. We can find strength and courage
in the promise that our good God is with us wherever
we go.

The LORD
your God is with
you wherever
you go.

ULTIMATE APPROVAL

The Kingdom of God is not a matter of what we eat or drink, but of living a life of goodness and peace and joy in the Holy Spirit. If you serve Christ with this attitude, you will please God, and others will approve of you, too.

ROMANS 14:17-18

Sometimes doing what pleases God also pleases others, especially godly people, but that is not always the case. Christ has many enemies who love evil more than good, so you may never earn their approval. Your ultimate purpose is to please the God who made you and redeemed you, no matter what others may think of you. Focus on him and seek his approval first; he promises that ultimately you will also receive the approval of those who sincerely love God.

LOVING GOD

*Those who accept my commandments and obey
them are the ones who love me. And because they
love me, my Father will love them. And I will
love them and reveal myself to each of them.*

JOHN 14:21

Like a father with his child, God is delighted
when you love him with all your heart and soul. He
loves it when you imitate his character by displaying
integrity, honesty, and purity of heart. When you obey
God, it shows him that you love him enough to trust
him with your life. God loved us first (see 1 John 4:10),
and each time you return his love through obedience,
he bathes you in ever deeper oceans of his truth
and love.

STRETCH YOUR ABILITIES

He takes no pleasure in the strength of a horse or in human might. No, the LORD's delight is in those who fear him, those who put their hope in his unfailing love.

PSALM 147:10-11

Does it comfort you to know that God is more impressed by your faith than your abilities? He uses your abilities in proportion to your faith. If you want to delight God, say yes to him, step out in faith, and watch him accomplish great things through you. Abilities give you the potential to do good; faith gives you the power to do good. Neither potential nor power alone is sufficient—they must work in harmony. Be inspired by God's unfailing love for you and for all he has made.

"THIS IS REAL LOVE"

God showed how much he loved us by sending his one and only Son into the world so that we might have eternal life through him. This is real love— not that we loved God, but that he loved us and sent his Son as a sacrifice to take away our sins.

1 JOHN 4:9-10

Real love is willing to sacrifice much—even life itself—for the good of someone else. You know for certain how much God loves you because he allowed Jesus to die in your place, to take the punishment for your sin so that you could be free from eternal judgment. Think of it: God allowed his Son to suffer terribly so that you could live forever with him. No wonder John wrote, "This is real love"!

BREATHE IN GOD'S PRESENCE

You go before me and follow me. You place your hand of blessing on my head. . . . I can never escape from your Spirit! I can never get away from your presence!

PSALM 139:5, 7

The Bible promises that God is always with those who love him. He is closer than the air we breathe. When you start looking for evidence of his presence with you, you will experience his companionship and receive his blessing.

Bathe Yourself in Love

Close your eyes and breathe in slowly, allowing your breath to fill your lungs completely. As you inhale, thank God for the gift of life. When you breathe out slowly, imagine exhaling your stress, anxiety, and tension. Do this several more times.

OUR BIG GOD

Oh, please help us against our enemies. . . .
With God's help we will do mighty things,
for he will trample down our foes.

PSALM 60:11-12

Try not to look at the size of your problem but at the size of your God. When there are so many seemingly impossible things to be done, remember that you have a powerful God who will help you triumph over all that seeks to keep you from accomplishing them. Call on the name of the Lord, and watch him move powerfully on your behalf.

With God's
help we will do
mighty things.

OVERFLOWING WITH GRATITUDE

*Give thanks for everything to God the Father
in the name of our Lord Jesus Christ.*

EPHESIANS 5:20

When you give thanks to God, you honor and
praise him for everything he has done. Similarly, when
you thank other people, you honor them and show
respect for who they are and what they have done. This
attitude of gratitude helps you serve others and allows
you to enjoy whatever blessings come your way. What
are you thankful for today?

Give thanks for
everything.

SOFTENED BY GOD'S CARE

I will be your God throughout your lifetime—until your hair is white with age. I made you, and I will care for you.

ISAIAH 46:4

The God who made you shows his care by protecting you and providing for your needs, as well as preserving you through life's difficulties. God's care softens your heart with gratefulness for his love and then inspires you to show the same care for others. You can protect, provide, and preserve by being kind, helpful, and willing to reach out; giving generously of your time, treasure, and talents; and maintaining harmony in relationships through your edifying words and actions.

YOUR MEANINGFUL LIFE

My life is worth nothing to me unless I use it for finishing the work assigned me by the Lord Jesus.

ACTS 20:24

You don't need to do earthshaking things in order to have a meaningful life. Your life has meaning when you do the work that God has given you to do. Whether you are changing diapers, running a company, or evangelizing the world, do it as though God were working through you—because he is! Your life has meaning because you are sharing the love of God with everyone in your circle of influence.

DUAL DELIGHT

The LORD your God will delight in you if you obey
his voice and keep the commands and decrees written
in this Book of Instruction, and if you turn to the
LORD your God with all your heart and soul.

DEUTERONOMY 30:10

Having a relationship with the Lord of the universe is an amazing thing. God blesses us in countless ways with his love, presence, and good gifts. But it's important to remember that a good relationship works in both directions. Can finite, sinful human beings truly bring joy and delight to the Lord, the Creator of the universe? God says yes! He created you because he wants to have a relationship with you, to delight in being with you. We can bring joy to God by honoring him with our trust, regular communication, honesty, humility, and service. Today, take the opportunity to invest in God's beautiful law of mutual delight.

BOOST YOUR CONFIDENCE

Those who are righteous will be long remembered.
They do not fear bad news; they confidently trust
the LORD to care for them. They are confident and
fearless and can face their foes triumphantly.

PSALM 112:6-8

Our confidence in others is built when they
demonstrate complete consistency between their words
and actions. Because God has never broken a single
promise in his Word—he has always done what he said
he would—arm yourself with the confidence that he'll
keep his promise to meet your needs and fight your
battles. You have nothing to fear, so give your confidence a boost and thank the Lord for his care.

QUIET MEDITATION

*I wait quietly before God, for my victory comes
from him. . . . Let all that I am wait quietly
before God, for my hope is in him.*

PSALM 62:1, 5

The practice of meditation involves setting aside
time to intentionally think about God, talk to him,
and listen to him. When you make time to meditate
on the Lord, you distance yourself from the distractions
and noise of the world and move within range of his
voice. You open your mind to his teaching and allow
him to mold your desires to reflect his own. As a result,
your thoughts and actions fall in line with his will.
Meditation is more than just the study of God. It is
intimate communion with him, which ultimately leads
to holy living.

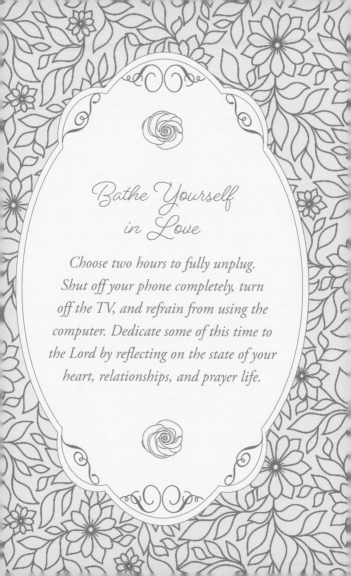

Bathe Yourself in Love

*Choose two hours to fully unplug.
Shut off your phone completely, turn
off the TV, and refrain from using the
computer. Dedicate some of this time to
the Lord by reflecting on the state of your
heart, relationships, and prayer life.*

DRENCHED IN SWEET FELLOWSHIP

Where two or three gather together as my
followers, I am there among them.

MATTHEW 18:20

We were created for community. Jesus commissioned the church to be a body of believers, not a collection of individuals. Isolation makes us vulnerable to discouragement and despair, so staying connected to other people in loving relationships helps us live with hope. When we're connected to a community of believers, we're able to worship together, support one another, and experience fellowship that keeps us strong in the faith, even during the most difficult times. This week, give yourself the gift of experiencing God's presence through fellowship with other believers.

Bathe Yourself in Love

Is there anyone in your church who can help you slow down or provide you with needed encouragement? Contact them today to schedule a time to talk or do something restful and restorative. For example, take a walk, play a game, or go out to dinner together.

SCRUB YOUR ATTITUDE

God is working in you, giving you the desire and the
power to do what pleases him. Do everything without
complaining and arguing, so that no one can criticize you.
Live clean, innocent lives as children of God, shining like
bright lights in a world full of crooked and perverse people.

PHILIPPIANS 2:13-15

Attitude is important because it affects your
thoughts, motives, and actions. As a Christian, you can
maintain a positive attitude because of the fact that the
God of the universe created you, loves you, and promises you eternal life. God is working for you, not against
you. Remind yourself of these truths each time you're
tempted to slip into negative thinking. Scrubbing your
attitude will transform the way you live and serve God.

God is working
in you.

A SAFE DIRECTION

Trust in the LORD with all your heart; do not depend on your own understanding. Seek his will in all you do, and he will show you which path to take.

PROVERBS 3:5-6

In order to receive good guidance, we have to know where to put our trust. For example, those who are traveling in unfamiliar territory must rely on accurate maps and signs to arrive at their destinations, and people who are critically ill must rely on medical experts to prescribe the proper treatments. In the same way, you must realize your own spiritual limitations and rely on the Bible—the instruction manual for life—in matters of faith. It's not possible for humans to understand all the complexities of life, but the Lord does. His Word will guide your decisions and show you the best way to live. Enjoy the direction and security he wants to provide.

He will show
you which
path to take.

ULTIMATE HEALING

He personally carried our sins in his body on the cross so that we can be dead to sin and live for what is right. By his wounds you are healed.

1 PETER 2:24

Sin is a disease that takes not only a physical, mental, and emotional toll but also a spiritual one. When we come to Jesus for treatment, he administers the antidote of his forgiveness. A miraculous healing takes place, and this disease can no longer control the way we live. But that's not the end of the story. Once we experience the Lord's forgiveness, we're compelled to forgive those who've hurt us, bringing even more spiritual healing into our lives. Ephesians 4:32 encourages us to "be kind to each other, tenderhearted, forgiving one another, just as God through Christ has forgiven [us]." Will you step out in faith today to receive God's gift of life and healing?

ANGELIC PROTECTION

He will order his angels to protect you wherever
you go. They will hold you up with their hands
so you won't even hurt your foot on a stone.

PSALM 91:11-12

The Bible doesn't say whether there is one
specific guardian angel assigned to each believer, but
it does say that God sends his angels to counsel, guide,
protect, minister to, rescue, fight for, and care for
his people. Whether he uses one specific angel or a
whole host of angels to help you is his choice and your
blessing. Chances are that angels have played a greater
role in your life than you realize. Thank God today for
the supernatural ways he cares for you.

ABUNDANT MERCY

His anger lasts only a moment,
but his favor lasts a lifetime!

PSALM 30:5

The Bible promises that God is kind and merciful and will always be ready to receive you with love when you confess your sins and seek a relationship with him. One of the worst caricatures of God is the image of him as an angry old man. Instead of harboring fierce anger and raining down cruel punishment, God corrects his children with gentle discipline that is actually an expression of his love in action.

INFUSED WITH FORGIVENESS

Oh, what joy for those whose disobedience is forgiven,
whose sins are put out of sight. Yes, what joy for
those whose record the LORD has cleared of sin.

ROMANS 4:7-8

Guilt is a legitimate spiritual response to sin, while regret is sorrow over the consequences of our decisions, both the sinful and the simply unfortunate. God promises to remove the guilt of all who seek his forgiveness, but he does not usually prevent the consequences of sin. Often we carry regret over those consequences and allow it to weigh us down with remorse. God promises to help you deal with your regret so you can move into the future without its heavy burden. He completely gets rid of your sin, so don't take it back by hanging on to regrets. Instead, let the Lord infuse you with the assurance of his forgiveness.

ENJOY THIS MOMENT

*You will show me the way of life, granting me the joy of
your presence and the pleasures of living with you forever.*

PSALM 16:11

It's true that the Bible acknowledges problems
will come our way. But God does promise lasting joy
for all who sincerely follow him. When you put your
trust in him, you can live daily with the assurance that
the God of the universe loves you, wants to know you,
will comfort and care for you, and has guaranteed
your eternal future with him. This kind of joy stays
with you despite your problems, and it helps you get
through them without being overwhelmed. It helps you
live in the moment instead of fretting about what's to
come. Simply bask in the Lord's presence as you savor
his gifts and the promises of his love and care.

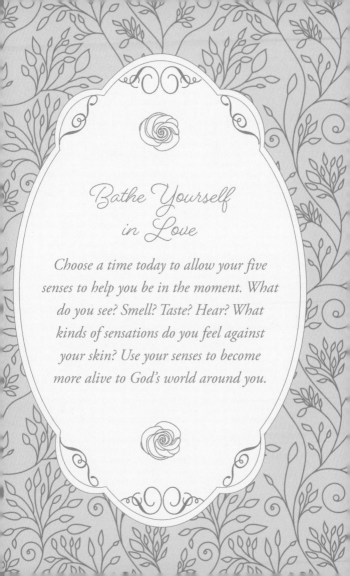

Bathe Yourself
in Love

*Choose a time today to allow your five
senses to help you be in the moment. What
do you see? Smell? Taste? Hear? What
kinds of sensations do you feel against
your skin? Use your senses to become
more alive to God's world around you.*

FORTIFIED BY GOD'S GRACE

[The Lord] said, "My grace is all you need. My power works best in weakness." So now I am glad to boast about my weaknesses, so that the power of Christ can work through me. That's why I take pleasure in my weaknesses, and in the insults, hardships, persecutions, and troubles that I suffer for Christ. For when I am weak, then I am strong.

2 CORINTHIANS 12:9-10

The more we recognize our weaknesses and limitations, the more we understand God's power at work within us. Feeling strong can make us proud and self-sufficient. But when we're weak and weary, we have no choice but to depend on God to work through us. Then there is no doubt that it is by his power—not our own—that the task is accomplished. Today, will you exchange your weaknesses for God's help and strength? His grace is all you need.

My grace is
all you need.

PURITY OF HEART

God blesses those whose hearts are
pure, for they will see God.

MATTHEW 5:8

Doctors urge us to exercise and eat nutritious
food to keep our hearts fit and healthy. In the Bible, the
heart is considered to be the center of thought and feeling. It's so important that God cautions you to guard
it "above all else" because "it determines the course
of your life" (Proverbs 4:23). When you receive Jesus
as the Lord of your life, he washes your heart clean.
But since your heart filters everything that happens to
you and around you, it's important to stay away from
anything that would cause it to become clogged with
all kinds of foulness—bitterness, jealousy, and impure
thoughts. When you follow the promptings of his
Spirit, he helps you avoid the toxins that lead to sinful
thoughts and desires that could destroy you. A pure
heart is the best prescription for a joyful and spiritually
healthy life.

God blesses
those whose
hearts are pure.

GLIMPSES OF THE ETERNAL

*God . . . has planted eternity in the human
heart, but even so, people cannot see the whole
scope of God's work from beginning to end.*

ECCLESIASTES 3:11

God has "planted eternity in the human heart." This
means that in our earthly existence, we instinctively
know there is something missing—that there's more
than just this life. Because we are created in God's
image, we have eternal value, and nothing but the
eternal God can truly satisfy us. He has built into us
a restless yearning for the kind of perfect world that
can only be found in heaven. He gives us a glimpse of
that world in the beauty of nature that we experience
here on earth. Someday he will restore the earth to the
splendor it had when he first created it. Eternity will
be a never-ending exploration of its glory in a perfect
relationship with God.

FILL UP WITH GOD'S WISDOM

Come and listen to my counsel. I'll share my heart with you and make you wise.

PROVERBS 1:23

God promises that if you listen to him, you will become wise. There are three ways you can listen to God: (1) *Pray.* Prayer is not just talking to God; it is also listening to him talk to you. (2) *Read the Bible.* God's Word is your instruction manual for living, with advice and wisdom about how the world works and how to navigate its many ups and downs. (3) *Listen to godly advice.* People who have experienced what you're going through can offer their wisdom about how to handle the situation, saving you much pain and heart-ache. Be encouraged by the many opportunities the Lord offers you for gaining wisdom and hearing from his heart.

CHOOSE PEACE

You will keep in perfect peace all who trust in you, all whose thoughts are fixed on you!

ISAIAH 26:3

There are many ways people try to achieve peace, but genuine peace is found only in a trusting relationship with God. Peace is not the absence of conflict but the presence of God. Peace of mind comes as the Holy Spirit guides you into God's purposes for your life and gives you an eternal perspective. Peace of heart comes as the Holy Spirit guides you into a productive life and comforts you in times of trouble. Be blessed with the Lord's peace today as you think about how wonderful he is.

BASK IN HIS FAITHFULNESS

If we are unfaithful, he remains faithful,
for he cannot deny who he is.

2 TIMOTHY 2:13

Who are you really—deep down inside?
Do you really love others? Are you truly faithful to
your family and friends? Faithfulness is necessary for
maintaining love because even those we hold closest to
our hearts will occasionally disappoint us. In the same
way, there are times when we're unfaithful to God. But
even when we fail him, God loves us and remains faithful to his promises. How incredible that even "if we are
unfaithful, he remains faithful." That's a pretty amazing
deal, don't you think? God's love for us is profound.
Model that same love to others by remaining faithful to
them even when they fail you. Your steadfastness will
show that your love is genuine.

EXPERIENCE INTIMACY WITH GOD

*Even when I walk through the darkest valley, I will
not be afraid, for you are close beside me. Your
rod and your staff protect and comfort me.*

PSALM 23:4

Intimacy with God helps you see his personal
touch in your everyday life. He is your Creator and
Shepherd. He wants to communicate with you, care
for you, advise you, and impart to you his joy and
blessings. When you walk with him and stay close to
his heart, he guides you step-by-step and offers his
comfort and protection. Look for him as you go about
your day, and you will see him right there beside you.

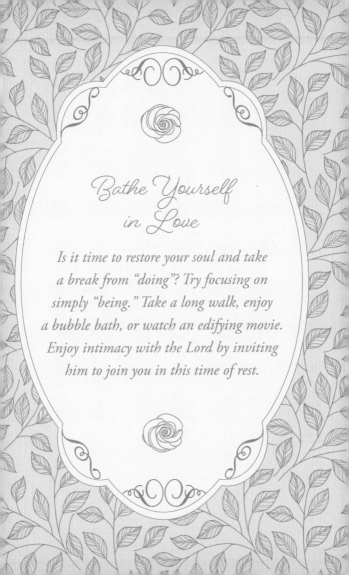

Bathe Yourself
in Love

*Is it time to restore your soul and take
a break from "doing"? Try focusing on
simply "being." Take a long walk, enjoy
a bubble bath, or watch an edifying movie.
Enjoy intimacy with the Lord by inviting
him to join you in this time of rest.*

YOUR UNCONTESTED VICTORY

If God is for us, who can ever be against us?

ROMANS 8:31

The forces of evil can't stand Jesus or even bear to hear his name. If you're living so that others will clearly see Jesus in you, there is bad news and good news. The bad news is that you will face opposition and even persecution for your faith. Satan opposes Jesus, so Satan is your enemy too. The good news is that even when the whole world is against you, God is for you. He promises to give you spiritual victories in this life and ultimate, eternal victory in his heavenly Kingdom.

Bathe Yourself
in Love

Today, commemorate a small victory
in your life. Perhaps you made a healthy
choice, finally finished a burdensome
task, or kept a boundary you set.
Celebrate by doing something you
enjoy. For example, go to dinner with
a friend, buy the good ice cream, or
curl up and relax with a good book.

ENRICHED BY JOY

Don't be dejected and sad, for the joy
of the LORD is your strength!

NEHEMIAH 8:10

The Bible says that God's very own joy will strengthen your heart. Joy springs from God's love, which is not dependent on your circumstances or your performance. When you realize just how great God's love for you really is, you become less vulnerable to depression and despair. The more you love him and become like him, the greater your joy will be. You will find perfect and lasting joy only in heaven, but you can still experience satisfying joy in this life by walking with God.

The joy of the
LORD is your
strength!

THE CYCLE OF BLESSING

Give, and you will receive. Your gift will return to you in full—pressed down, shaken together to make room for more, running over, and poured into your lap. The amount you give will determine the amount you get back.

LUKE 6:38

The act of giving creates a cycle of blessing. As God generously provides for your needs, you have the opportunity to give back to him as well as to others. This in turn inspires those you've blessed to offer their time, finances, or goods to God's work and to people in need. God promises that when you give, you will receive a blessing in return. What can you do today to start a cycle of abundant giving?

Give, and you
will receive.

FUEL FOR GROWTH

You will grow as you learn to know God better and better. We also pray that you will be strengthened with all his glorious power so you will have all the endurance and patience you need.

COLOSSIANS 1:10-11

The fuel you need for growth can be found by seeking to know God better and letting his power work in you. As you become more obedient and more in tune with God, he will strengthen you—not just to endure, but to persevere with joy!

SUSTAINING SATISFACTION

*Those who drink the water I give will never be
thirsty again. It becomes a fresh, bubbling spring
within them, giving them eternal life.*

JOHN 4:14

Everyone is searching for something to
quench their thirsting souls. But too many people try
to fill their lives with the wrong things. The key is to
fill yourself with something that will last. God promises
that when you saturate your heart and mind with his
Word and his Spirit, you'll be equipped with the tools
and hope you need to overcome the trials of this world.
Such a life will endow you with true, lasting, eternal
satisfaction.

LET COMFORT SURROUND YOU

*All praise to God, the Father of our Lord Jesus Christ.
God is our merciful Father and the source of all
comfort. He comforts us in all our troubles so that we
can comfort others. When they are troubled, we will be
able to give them the same comfort God has given us.*

2 CORINTHIANS 1:3-4

It's easy to look to people or things to comfort
us in our distress. But God's Word tells us that he alone
is the true source of comfort. God's assuring love, his
guiding wisdom, and his sustaining power will carry
us through our troubles. And one day, our experience
of God's comfort will help us comfort others.

REMEMBER WHAT HE'S DONE

*Remember the things I have done in the past. For
I alone am God! I am God, and there is none like me.*

ISAIAH 46:9

It's easy to forget about things that aren't important to you, so be sure to give God utmost importance
in your life. Then you will more likely remember how
you have seen the Lord at work in the past, and you'll
go to him first when you need help again. You can keep
your focus on God by telling others what he is doing in
your life now, by meditating on his Word to discover
how he has worked throughout history, and by sharing
his blessings and promises with the next generation.
When you do these things, you help yourself and others
acknowledge God's hand in the past and live with the
hope that his faithfulness will sustain you in the present
and the future.

SEEING BEYOND TODAY

*We don't look at the troubles we can see now;
rather, we fix our gaze on things that cannot be
seen. For the things we see now will soon be gone,
but the things we cannot see will last forever.*

2 CORINTHIANS 4:18

God promises that the troubles looming in front of you won't last forever. Your goal, then, is to turn your focus away from them and look instead toward those things that will last forever—God's love, his gift of salvation, his care, and your eternal future with him. When you live with this perspective, you see your hurts and troubles as part of this temporary world, and you take comfort in knowing they won't last. It doesn't diminish the fact that your struggles are difficult, but you can rest in a more real and lasting promise: the hope of a world with no more pain. Will you allow this encouraging truth to soak into your heart today?

Bathe Yourself in Love

Get into a comfortable position and allow each part of your body to relax, from the muscles in your face all the way down to your toes. Notice where you hold your tension, and try to let it go.

GET INVIGORATED

It is good to give thanks to the LORD,
to sing praises to the Most High.

PSALM 92:1

When you praise the Lord, it lifts your mood. Such a deliberate act of worship may be hard to engage in when you're feeling down, but it produces almost immediate results. Praise the Lord for his unfailing, unconditional love for you. Praise him for the gift of salvation and eternal life. Praise him for his promise to help you through your hard times. Praise him for anything good you see around you. Prepare to be invigorated!

It is good to
give thanks to
the LORD.

AN OPEN INVITATION

Learn to know the God of your ancestors intimately.
Worship and serve him with your whole heart and a
willing mind. For the LORD sees every heart and knows
every plan and thought. If you seek him, you will find him.

1 CHRONICLES 28:9

Remember that God is with you all day,
every day, so talk to him about everything that comes
up at home, at work, or in any area of your life. Share
your thoughts, needs, and concerns with him. As you
practice acknowledging his presence, you'll begin to
gain the intimacy you desire.

If you seek
him, you will
find him.

NOTES

_____

_____

_____

_____

_____

_____

_____

_____

_____

_____

_____

_____

_____

_____

_____

_____

_____